DASHBOARD SELLING

The Systematic, Repeatable approach for driving more sales.

ROBERT BEASLEY

ISBN: 0983432805
ISBN-13: 9780983432807

Thanks to my wife Leslie for the enthusiastic and unending encouragement.

This book is for all the salespeople who have a deep desire to excel at their profession. My hope is that Dashboard Selling will help you become a true master of your craft. As you make your way down the road to sales success, I encourage you to find someone who is in need and extend a helping hand. I can assure you that you'll enjoy a greater reward when you share your time, money and talents with other people. Best of luck as you begin the process of becoming a Dashboard Selling enthusiast!

Table of Contents

PREFACE

We live in a world that is quickly drowning in information. There are mountains of paper everywhere and millions of computers filled to the rim with information on every subject under the sun. Buried somewhere under these piles of data is a priceless supply of information on selling skills. If we were completely honest, we'd all agree that hardworking salespeople don't have the time to read a book that requires 250 pages to make the point. If it takes hundreds of pages to explain a concept, it won't likely be usable in any real-life selling situation. With that in mind, this book is designed to communicate the sales methodology in a concise and easily-accessible format. We're going to move quickly, so buckle your seatbelt and get ready to learn the fastest and most effective way to improve your sales results.

As you blaze through it, I guarantee you'll find…
…no fluff.
…no long-winded stories of my great lifetime sales achievements to impress you.
…no nonsense.
…just the facts.

Dashboard Selling will tell you WHAT to do and HOW to do it in plain English.

It's art.
It's science.
It works.

INTRODUCTION

Everywhere you turn there is noise. Cars, TVs, radios, MP3 players, cell phones, emails, text messages, magazines, billboards, banner ads, junk mail, etc. Created to inform and entertain us, this stuff is cluttering our minds, clouding our thoughts and distracting us from what matters. The world of sales has its own share of noise too. Wave after wave of tips, tricks, techniques, philosophies, prospect pushback and manager mandates get us chasing our tails instead of focusing on the things that actually influence winning and losing deals. In too many sales organizations, salespeople are under so much pressure to justify and report on what they're doing, they run out of time to sell. I have seen way too many gifted salespeople bail on the profession because their daily activities have become such a grind. That might make you happy because it thins the competitive field, but remember: without a new approach, the grind will get you too.

That new approach is Dashboard Selling, a systematic, repeatable approach for driving more sales. It will help you objectively <u>assess</u> each sales opportunity to determine exactly what <u>questions</u> you need to ask and what <u>actions</u> you need to take to improve your probability of winning deals. The Dashboard is the unbiased, ultimate truth-teller that will clear your head and help you quickly jump on the steps you should take to win the deal.

Dashboard Selling will also help you articulate the essential information your manager needs to know about your pipeline without devouring your precious selling time. Dashboard Selling moves you out from under the microscope and into the driver's seat, with control of your deals, a better upside for your boss and more money in your pocket in less time.

If you've worked your way up to sales manager, Dashboard Selling will give you a structure to assess your salespeople's efforts and opportunities without those teeth-pulling games of twenty questions.

If you're still reading at this point, it's safe to assume you're ready to get rolling, so here goes.

DASHBOARD
SELLING
OVERVIEW

If you've been in the sales trenches for a while, most of the high-level concepts within Dashboard Selling should be familiar since selling has been around since the first caveman traded a smooth stone for a piece of charred meat. While new methods, approaches, challenges and mediums will continue to emerge, there are some things that never change in the world of selling. Dashboard Selling is based on the time-tested notion that every sales opportunity features 12 key indicators you must successfully manage to close.

In any transaction, a salesperson must:

1) Ask <u>questions</u> to determine the status of each key indicator.

2) Take specific <u>actions</u> to favorably influence each indicator.

Regardless of its meaning elsewhere, Q&A in selling means Questions and Actions…it's that easy.

The key is asking the <u>right</u> questions then taking the <u>right</u> actions based on the answers. The positive answers might make you happy, but your focus must be directed toward exception management. Using exception management, your attention, energy and effort must be devoted to capturing missing information and changing negative information. (This approach is similar to the Six Sigma approach that has transformed manufacturing and other business processes around the world. In short, Six Sigma is about removing defects and minimizing variability from processes, whether you're building minivans or selling widgets.)

As a Dashboard Seller, your goal is to remove defects and minimize the negative variables that affect your sales opportunities. If you improve your process management, devote more time to managing exceptions, you'll produce better sales results. It doesn't sound glamorous, but minimizing variability in your approach to every sales opportunity will yield constant improvements.

The Opportunity Dashboard

Let's tackle the basics first, starting with the 12 indicators. In a display of either bizarre coincidence or cosmic convergence, they each begin with the letter "P". (That makes them pretty easy to remember too.) Take some time to memorize these key things that must occur for an organization to make a purchase. If you become an expert at them, you will be unstoppable. The indicators are:

Pain
Priority
Payback
Payment
Process
Preferences
Positioning
Proof
People (there are 4 indicators for this label)

Here's a sneak-peek at the Opportunity Dashboard. If it helps, imagine it is part of the heads up display in a fighter jet, giving you the essential information you need to hit your target.

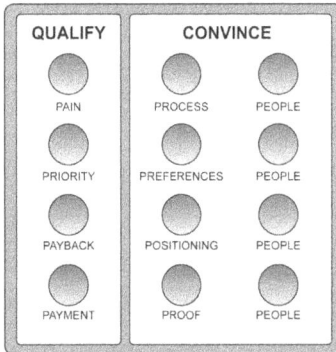

As you learn to read the Opportunity Dashboard, you'll learn that indicators won't necessarily light up in sequence or be fully illuminated by the end of your first discussion. However, your goal is to energize every light in the dashboard in successive conversations with your prospect as you fill in the blanks in your understanding.

In the following chapters, we'll coach you to mastery of the dashboard in three steps:

A) SECTION 1: Clearly define each indicator.

B) SECTION 2: Provide sample questions that will uncover the information you need about each indicator.

C) <u>SECTION 3</u>: Describe specific <u>actions</u> that will affect the status of each indicator.

Note: We will use the word "solution" throughout the book to indicate the entirety of what a customer receives when they make a purchase from your company. This includes your products, services, company value, you, your team, etc.

DEFINITIONS
OVERVIEW

On the following pages, you will find clear, concise definitions of each indicator on the Opportunity Dashboard which are the methodology's fundamental building blocks. To get the most out of Dashboard Selling you must not only commit these concepts to memory, but also eliminate any preconceived notions of what each indicator represents. There are essential elements of each definition you must understand and embrace before moving into the Questions and Actions sections. The improvement of your sales results will be directly tied to how thoroughly you incorporate the Dashboard into your daily routine.

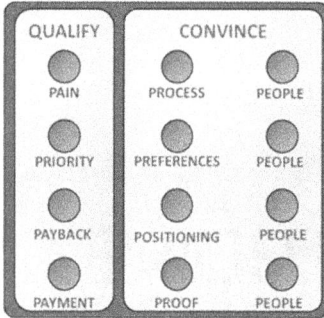

As you can see, the indicators on the Dashboard are broken into two categories: QUALIFY and CONVINCE.

The QUALIFY indicators show <u>if</u> a prospect is going to buy.

The CONVINCE indicators determine <u>who</u> the prospect will buy from.

In short, you need to make sure you have a <u>qualified</u> buyer before you start <u>convincing</u> them you have the best solution. Premature selling is one of the fastest ways to frustrate and alienate a prospect.

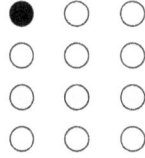

CHAPTER 1:
PAIN DEFINITION

All of your sales hopes and dreams are contingent upon one thing: finding and helping people who have Pain. A prospect will make a strategic purchase to address specific <u>issues</u> that are causing them significant Pain, whether it's a problem or an opportunity. Your job is to identify it and enable them to safely acknowledge it. Without that, they're not likely to buy anything.

It's tragic to consider how many salespeople waste their precious time calling, emailing, having meetings and completing to-dos for prospects that don't have or won't acknowledge pain.

For strategic purchases, you and the prospect must understand what is <u>causing</u> the pain and how that pain is <u>impacting</u> their key business drivers. There are several common key business drivers for most organizations: their customers, their financials, their competitors, their organizational goals, their employees and their business partners. You and the prospect need to know how the specific pain is impacting some/all of these areas. If you commit these common key business drivers to memory, you can sit down with anyone, anytime and drill, drill, drill until you hit the pain.

<u>**Summary**</u>: Lighting up the Pain indicator requires you to:

- Uncover the <u>issues</u> that are causing the prospect pain
- Identify the <u>causes</u> of the issues
- Zero in on the <u>impact</u> the pain is having on the prospect's key business drivers.

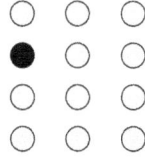

CHAPTER 2:
PRIORITY DEFINITION

Once you uncover a significant Pain, it's time to address the notion of Priority. While the prospect may have pain, they still might not engage in a buying cycle because solving that problem isn't a priority for them right now.

In today's business world, everyone has more things on their to-do list than they have time to conquer. So, the only things that get done are the ones at the top of the list. Any number of things could be taking the top spot from the pain you've identified. You'll waste a lot of time and effort if you don't confirm that their pain is a top priority. If it is, you'll be dealing with a ready, willing and able buyer.

For something to be a priority for an organization, there must be an <u>owner</u> who is taking responsibility for its resolution. Someone on the client side needs to have some "skin in the game" and the accompanying willingness to invest the time and political capital needed to rally the troops and solve it. This is a lot harder than it sounds because a lot of people spend their workday doing the smallest acceptable amount of work before they bail at 4:59pm every day. Since the can of worms you want to open up might keep them away from their bowling league, they might be happier just ignoring some Pains.

If the stars align and someone in the organization takes ownership of finding a solution, it won't move forward until someone with the proper level of authority declares it an official <u>project</u>. If the problem's owner lacks the authority to initiate a project, they'll have to garner support from other folks within the organization to gain project status.

Our best case scenario also requires a <u>deadline</u> for the project's completion. Hard and fast deadlines don't always exist, but you need one to act as a backstop or finish line for your sales cycle. No deadline means the deal is likely to slip, and slip and slip and slip.

Summary: Lighting up the Priority indicator requires the following:

- Someone has become the <u>owner</u> of solving the Pain
- An official <u>project</u> has been initiated to solve the Pain
- There is a <u>deadline</u> for completing the project

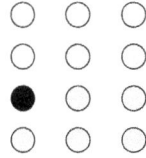

CHAPTER 3:
PAYBACK
DEFINITION

If you've knocked Pain and Priority out of the park, pat yourself on the back and get ready to tackle the next indicator: Payback. Also known as "value" or "return", Payback comes in two forms: quantitative and qualitative. Quantitative values are things you can measure like revenue, expenses, headcount, inventory levels and employee productivity. Qualitative value is harder to measure but equally important. Things like reduced frustration, status of using a particular solution, potential for promotion, perception of risk and job satisfaction can affect buying decisions. Like the dangling carrot that keeps the mule walking forward, you and your prospect must share a clear understanding of the Payback, because that's what makes investing the time, money and resources worthwhile.

Payback is the real incentive and, if the right people within the prospect's account don't believe it is significant and they will actually receive it when the deal closes, the deal will eventually die before your eyes. (Ouch!) If you look back over the sales opportunities that never made it over the finish line, you'll likely find that this key element was missing. Even with Pain, a prospect won't move forward unless they believe the Payback is worth the investment.

Prospects don't view your solution's Payback in a vacuum. Instead, they are constantly evaluating the Payback of fixing multiple problems at the same time in the context of limited dollars and limited time. The Pain they think will deliver the greatest Payback with the least amount of effort is usually the one they'll pick. Your job is to capture and summarize quantitative and qualitative Payback in a document that you share with the prospect. Then you need to have the prospect validate that they believe your solution will deliver the Payback you defined. We'll show you how later in the book.

Summary: Lighting up the Payback indicator requires you to:

- Identify <u>Quantitative</u> Payback related to things like: revenue, expenses, profit, head-count, etc.
- Identify <u>Qualitative</u> Payback related to things like: satisfaction, ease, reputation, etc.
- Provide a <u>document</u> summarizing the Payback for the prospect
- <u>Validate</u> that the prospect believes the Payback is attainable.

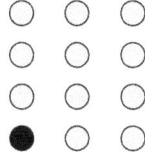

CHAPTER 4:
PAYMENT
DEFINITION

Even if a prospect becomes utterly convinced they would receive a generous Payback for solving a particular problem, they won't necessarily purchase a solution. They could be hung up on the issue of resources, identifying a source of funds to invest in the problem's resolution. This is what we call Payment. ("What?! You mean we actually have to pay for the dang thing?")

There are several things you need to nail down when it comes to Payment. First, the prospect must have <u>budget</u> available to invest in your solution. Chances are they haven't officially budgeted for your solution, but that can be overcome if they can get to the necessary funds. Second, the amount of money they're willing to invest should be in the <u>ballpark</u> of your solution's costs. The nicest prospect in the world can still break your heart (and waste your time) if their promised budget ends up short a few zeroes at the end of the number. So affirm that the investment they expect to make is in the right range for your solution. Being within plus or minus 20% is usually close enough, because you should be able to close the gap through stellar selling skills and some final negotiations.

Finally, you need to identify the actual <u>owner</u> of the budget. This not only helps you affirm that the budget dollars actually exist, it'll also indicate where a large portion of the decision making influence resides.

<u>Summary</u>: Lighting up the Payment indicator requires you to:

- Confirm that the prospect has <u>budget</u>
- Assure that their budget amount is in the right <u>ballpark</u> for your solution
- Identify the <u>owner</u> of the budget

Ding Ding

If you've nailed the first four Dashboard indicators, you can pat yourself on the back. You now have what Dashboard Selling defines as a qualified buyer. A qualified buyer is someone who, unless the sky falls, he or she gets fired or hell freezes over, is going to buy something. Now it's just a matter of <u>who</u> they are going to buy it from. As you move them toward making that who you, remember we don't live in a perfect world.

That means remember that plenty of opportunities progress far into the sales cycle without meeting all of the qualification criteria. For example, a buyer may not identify the funds to satisfy the Payment indicator until they are 80% of the way through their purchasing process. So it goes. Your goal as a salesperson is to manage toward the best case scenario (in which the Payment indicator is satisfied early in the sales cycle) knowing it may not happen every time. Just do your best and let the Dashboard be your guide.

When you first look at the Dashboard, with nothing illuminated, you have a "Prospect". Once the first column of indicators shows positive, the prospect is officially "qualified" and has graduated to "Buyer" status. This allows you to focus the majority of your efforts on selling. (Yeah!) The remaining indicators will guide you through the process of convincing the Buyer that your solution is best suited to address their Pain.

"Convincing" is essentially the art of influencing people. "Coercing" is something entirely different and Dashboard Selling prevents you from having to manipulate or force people into buying. That just leaves them feeling abused, no matter how great your product or service is. Instead, be positive and influence buyers with the way you manage each interaction with them and your approach to describing the positive aspects of your solution. Your influence in sales flows out of your personal credibility with the buyer.

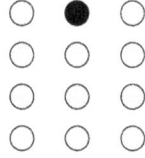

CHAPTER 5:
PROCESS DEFINITION

A good salesperson starts by learning the process a buyer will complete on the way to a purchase. Understanding the decision making <u>steps</u> a buyer will take enables you to prepare. Conversely, if you don't know what steps they'll take, you'll end up confused, unprepared and less effective at influencing the buyer.

Unless you're selling to a tiny startup, most buyers follow fairly standard purchasing processes. Once you uncover the steps a buyer will take, you need to find out what <u>people</u> will be involved in each step and the expected <u>timeline</u> for completing each step. This knowledge will help you apply the timeless Boy Scout saying: "always be prepared".

Summary: Lighting up the Process indicator requires you to:

- Identify the <u>steps</u> the buyer will take to make the purchase
- Know which <u>people</u> will be involved in each step
- Gain agreement on a <u>timeline</u> for completing each step in the process

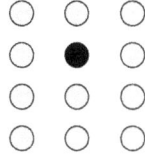

CHAPTER 6:
PREFERENCES DEFINITION

eople can be wildly diverse, but they generally share one trait in common: they all
have opinions. Your prospects are no exception.
In fact they're paid to have informed opinions,
otherwise, they won't last long in their jobs.
On the Dashboard, these "opinions" are called
"preferences" and they represent the "buying
criteria" used by customers to select a solution.
Buyers generally don't make a purchase until
they have a clear set of buying criteria and a solution that aligns reasonably well with them.

Uncovering their <u>criteria</u> will allow you to communicate the benefits of your solution as they

align with those preferences. Furthermore, you need to know the relative importance of each buying criteria within their purchase equation.

Discerning the <u>weight</u> they attach to each criterion will allow you to zero in on their priorities as you position your solution. If you don't know their criteria, you'll shoot in the dark until they cut you off…unless you accidentally say something that connects with one of their hot buttons.

Interestingly, as a credible salesperson, you can actually influence the buying criteria. Sometimes you need to try to <u>adjust</u> the buyer's criteria when they've omitted aspects that are strengths of your solution (or when they seem fixated on criteria that don't play to your strengths.)

Once you've developed a thorough understanding of the buyer's criteria and done your best to adjust their criteria to play to your strengths, it is time to <u>align</u> your solution to their criteria. Generic pitches don't connect the dots, but custom-crafted pitches can really move the numbers.

Summary: Lighting up the Preferences indicator requires you to:

- Identify their buying <u>criteria</u>
- Determine the <u>weight</u> of each criteria (what are the "must haves")
- Try to <u>adjust</u> their criteria to play to your strengths
- <u>Align</u> your solution to their criteria

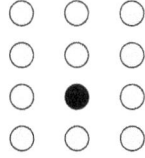

CHAPTER 7:
POSITIONING DEFINITION

Sometimes, you may be cruising along with a clear picture of the buyer's Preferences and a solution that cleanly aligns with their Preferences, but doubt will nag at you, because your picture is incomplete. Experience tells you there is more to the equation ...right?

Just because your solution can actually solve their problem and has everything they need doesn't mean you're going to win the deal. You can't forget that crucial element: your competitors. In fact, you need to know them as well as you know yourself so you can properly position yourself against them. While your offering may align just fine with the buyer's criteria, one of your competitors may stack up better. You need to know how the buyer views your solution in relation to the other solutions they're considering so you can positively influence their perception.

It doesn't matter how your solution <u>actually</u> compares to your competitors' solutions. It only matters how the prospect <u>perceives</u> your solutions. We've all heard the saying "perception is reality" and it's never more true than in sales. Your solution may actually be 10 times better than your competitor, but that doesn't matter if your prospect doesn't think so.

You need to figure out your buyer's perception of the <u>strengths</u> and <u>weaknesses</u> you and your competitors bring to the table. Any advantage your competitors have on you would be indicated on the Positioning indicator.

<u>**Summary**</u>: Lighting up the Positioning indicator requires you to:

- Know the buyer's perception of yours and your competitors' <u>strengths</u> and <u>weaknesses</u>

- <u>Emphasize</u> your strengths and <u>minimize</u> your weaknesses
- Find out if the buyer has one of your a competitors in a better Position to win

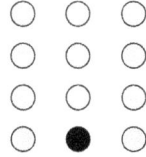

CHAPTER 8:
PROOF
DEFINITION

The indicator missed most often during a sales cycle is Proof. Salespeople tend to think that if they've told the buyer the facts about their solution and/or promised them they'll get specific results, then the buyer automatically believes them. In case you have this nonsense flowing through your mind, here's a little news alert:

Buyers are suspicious of pretty much everything that comes out of your mouth.

Like it or not, it's a fact of life for salespeople, even in the twenty-first century. For that fact, we can thank all of the dishonest snake oil salesmen that came before us. This reality means you must provide compelling proof to back up each of your major claims, most of which are directly related to the other "P"s of Dashboard Selling.

You need to offer some strong evidence to demonstrate A) the <u>Payback</u> your solution will deliver B) the way your solution aligns to their <u>Preferences</u> C) your solution's <u>Positioning</u> compared to the other solutions they're considering.

After delivering proof sources for each of these areas, you need to validate their legitimacy in the eyes of your prospect. Providing solid Proof will increase your influence on the buyer and ratchet up your odds of winning the business.

Summary: Lighting up the Proof indicator requires you to:

- Give evidence that your solution will actually deliver the <u>Payback</u> you communicated
- Demonstrate that your solution aligns to their most important <u>Preferences</u>
- Substantiate any <u>Positioning</u> claims you've made relative to your competitors
- <u>Validate</u> that the prospect accepts the Proof sources you've provided

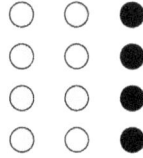

CHAPTER 9:
PEOPLE
DEFINITION

Last but not least in this process is People. They will ultimately determine whether you win or lose the deal. A quick glance at the Opportunity Dashboard reveals the importance of People, because they merit four indicators on this category. The People aspect to Dashboard Selling is about four times more important than each of the other aspects.

All of the other "P"s position you to gain the support of the right people. All the stars can be aligned on the other Dashboard indicators and you can lose the deal in a nano-second if you haven't covered your bases with the right people.

If you've been selling for more than a week, you already know this. Depending on the nature of your solution, you may have one or two people involved in the decision or you may have a dozen. Either way, this simple approach will help you.

Your job is to convince the people with the most influence that your solution is best suited to their preferences. The key in the previous sentence is "most influence". Salespeople tend to spend too much time with people who don't have the most influence on the decision. To help you stay focused, Dashboard Selling isolates three types of people. (Approver, Recommender & Influencer). In large accounts with complex sales cycles, there may be multiple people in some of these categories. In this case, you should focus on the top person in each category. Most of the time, you will win over everyone if you gain the favor of the most influential people. Following is a detailed description of the three types of people in Dashboard Selling.

Recommender

The recommender is the project leader who drives the evaluation and ultimately puts forth their (or the team's) recommendation to someone else for approval. They can't move forward on the purchase without someone else's approval. That someone else is the "Approver."

Approver

People often call the Approver the Decision Maker. We use the label Approver because the so-called Decision Maker doesn't always make the decision on WHICH solution is purchased. Instead, they decide IF a solution will be purchased. The so-called "decision maker" may not even be involved in evaluating the solutions or deciding which one is best for the organization. So, we apply the label "Approver" to make it clear that this person, whether they are involved in the evaluation or not, is the person who has the authority to say "yes" and execute the agreement.

Influencer

The last people category is Influencer. Influencers can come in many shapes and sizes. They can be users of the solution or technical experts. They might be consultants or they may be on the purchasing staff. Your main objective is to identify which influencers will have the greatest impact on your deal and make sure you purposefully court them.

The Dashboard isolates two Influencers and they're usually enough in most sales cycles. Many sales organizations "hard code" the roles/titles of the two influencers to increase the dashboard's clarity and specificity. For example, a software company selling to an IT organization might have the CIO as the Approver, the Director of IT as the Recommender, an Application Manager as one Influencer and a business user as a the second Influencer. This makes it very easy to see whether you have adequate coverage on the right people in the account.

In the Actions section, we will go into great detail about how you gain the favor of each person. In the meantime, the following summary will provide quick preview.

Summary: Lighting up the People indicators requires you to:

- <u>Identify</u> each of the people on the Dashboard
- Spend <u>time</u> with each person

- Determine and adapt to their <u>personality type</u>
- Identify their <u>top Preferences</u>
- Uncover and address their <u>concerns</u>
- Know the <u>personal impact</u> the purchase decision will have on them
- Get them to <u>endorse</u> the decision to purchase your solution

DEFINITIONS
SUMMARY

Having worked through the key components of the Sales Dashboard, some of you big stud salespeople might be saying "that's a nice little concept you have there but I already know about all that stuff".

Of course you do...but are you addressing "all that stuff" on every single deal?

Do you have a systematic way to diagnose each area? Do you use that approach each and every time you work on an opportunity? Do you have a methodical approach of responding based on what each indicator says? Do you use the same approach so often that you're getting better and better and better at selling?

You soon will.

Now that you have a solid understanding of what each indicator means, we will begin to explain how you manage the indicators. In the following sections, we'll provide QUESTIONS you can ask to capture the information you need on each indicator. Second, we'll provide recommendations on the ACTIONS you can take to influence each indicator. Prepare yourself to become armed and dangerous!

SECTION 2:

QUESTIONS

While working with sales teams, I spent years trying to avoid giving salespeople the specific words they should use to ask questions. As a sales trainee in my earlier career, I always found it frustrating when a trainer would unleash a litany of questions that, if asked in the **_exact_** right manner, promised to be the key to my sales success. Most of the questions seemed cheesy or not my style and I never could remember the **_exact_** right wording anyway. When I became a sales trainer, I felt like it was more important for salespeople to understand the key concepts then devise their own questions to get the information they needed. I felt that salespeople needed to invest in developing their own questions or they would never truly apply what they were learning.

I also believe that cooking up your own wording leads to questions that fit your unique style.

For years, I avoided handing out specific questions or phrases, but I was finally persuaded to change my perspective. In training sessions, salespeople ask "how would you ask a question to get that information"? When I would give them an off-the-cuff example, they would often say "oh yeah…I like the way you said that…that sounds good." As a part of our comprehensive sales force development programs, I do one-on-one coaching sessions with salespeople where I actually participate in their calls and meetings. Oftentimes, I'd get the same positive reaction when I would ask their prospects questions. So, I finally relented and decided to provide some of the verbiage I've found to be effective in my career.

I still hold firmly to the idea that each salesperson has to develop their communication skills, molding and shaping professional language into something that fits them. However, it doesn't hurt to use my questions as a starting point for your next stage of development. Detailed concepts and ideas about questioning and communication techniques will be addressed in another book, but one key lesson from this book is this: the <u>way</u> you ask a question can often determine whether you get the information you're looking for. Many salespeople ask the same old questions in the same old way and get the same old (less than stellar) results. They ask questions in a way that immediately triggers prospects' "cheesy salesperson alarm" which causes them to shut down and start guarding information.

You have to purge any language that makes you sound like a salesperson and replace it with language that makes you sound like a business person. Listening to CEOs speak and reading the letters to shareholders in annual reports will help you get a better feel for the type of language you should be using. The other thing you need to guard against is using too much marketing fodder in your verbal communication. Some words and phrases may look fine in print but sound very awkward when spoken. You can't expect to regurgitate the contents of a brochure or website verbatim and expect it to work. If you do, you can expect prospects' "get this guy out of my office" alarm to be going off throughout your visit.

In the following chapters, I provide a number of samples for your consideration. Examine them closely and notice the nuances of phrasing. Adapt these ideas to your own style and, before long, you'll find prospects more willing to share the information you need. While good grammar is necessary, don't lose track of the other channels you're using to communicate. Your tone, inflection and body language make a huge impact on how the question is received. Be conscious of the number of questions you ask at any one time. If you stroll in like a private detective on a mission to interrogate the prospect and sift through every shred of their dirty laundry, they will feel it and shut down on you. If you act casual and conversational yet professional, you'll have better luck, so don't expect to ask all the questions for every Dashboard indicator at one time. Pay attention to the prospect to gauge his or her openness and attitude toward you. Have a plan for what information you'll share in the gaps to give your prospect time to breathe, listen, take a sip of their coffee and get comfortable with you.

When necessary, we will provide sample questions to help you understand how to apply each type of question. For all of the sample questions, we will use the same scenario. The salesperson asking the question works for a software company that sells a sales force automation application. (Something all salespeople should be able to understand.)

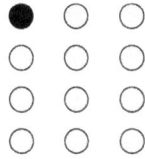

CHAPTER 10:
PAIN
QUESTIONS

Definition Reminder: You have to uncover issues that are causing the prospect significant pain in order to address them. If your solution is strategic to their organization and/or a significant financial investment, you and the prospect need to know what is <u>causing</u> it and how it is <u>impacting</u> their key business drivers (ie: customers, competitors, employees, partners, financials, goals, risk). The following questions can help you get that information and prepare to inflame the pain.

<u>Question 1</u>: I've talked to companies like yours and they seem to be experiencing issues with

<describe a pain that your solution addresses>.
Are you running into those issues too? Tell me a little about it.

> <u>Example</u>: It seems like a lot people I've talked to at companies like yours are experiencing issues with tracking sales team activities and forecasting revenue. Are you running into those issues too?

<u>Question 2</u>: It seems to me that <u>describe pain(s) that your solution addresses></u> can be a never ending battle. Are you focusing on that right now?

> <u>Example</u>: Making sure your sales reps are following up with prospects and making cold calls can be a never ending battle. Are you focusing on that right now?

<u>Question 3</u>: How is <u>describe pain(s) they've admitted to></u> impacting the key parts of your business like <u>list the most relevant key business drivers out of the following list (customers, financials, goals, competitors, employees, partners, risk)></u>?

Example: How is your inability to accurately forecast revenue impacting your company's financial projections for Wall Street?

Question 4: How would you rate your current solution on a scale of 1 to 10? What areas would need to be improved to move you to a 10?

Question 5: On a scale from 1 to 10, how good is your current solution at <u>describe capabilities of your solution</u>?

Example: On a scale from 1 to 10, how good is your current solution at automatically cultivating new leads that enter the system?

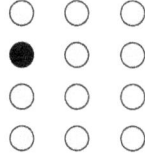

CHAPTER 11:
PRIORITY QUESTIONS

Definition **Reminder**: You must make sure the prospect is ready to engage in a buying cycle before you try to convince them that your solution is the best. There should be a person who has taken <u>ownership</u> of solving the problem. Someone with the appropriate level of authority should have initiated an official <u>project</u> and the project should have a <u>deadline</u> for completion. We will talk about how you influence the priority of your project in the Actions section.

<u>Question 1</u>: If you're like everyone else I know, you have more things on your to-do list than you

can possibly get done. Is solving this issue a top priority for you?

Question 2: This sounds like a fairly important issue to address. Are you ready to begin evaluating your alternatives right now?

Question 3: Has an official project been initiated to address this issue?

Question 4: What is the timeline associated with completing this project?

Question 5: What happens if you don't solve this problem by a certain date?

Question 6: Is someone in management going to care if this situation isn't improved?

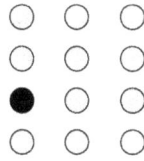

CHAPTER 12:
PAYBACK
QUESTIONS

Definition Reminder: The prospect has to be absolutely sure that they will receive a significant payback if they invest time and money to eliminate the pain. Payback comes in two forms: quantitative ("hard ROI") and qualitative ("soft ROI"). You can play an integral role in helping them identify and document the value. We will talk about how to communicate your solution's payback in the Actions section.

Question 1: <Describe pain(s) they are experiencing> is certainly impacting important parts of your organization. How would you quantify the value of solving this issue?

Example: Inability to see past activities on an account is certainly impacting important parts of your organization. How would you quantify the value of solving this issue?

Question 2: We've found that most of our customers have <u><state quantitative value></u>. Does that seem achievable at your organization? What do you think is possible?

Example: We've found that most of our customers have increased revenue per rep by 10% after implementing our sales force automation solution. Does that seem achievable at your organization? What do you think is possible?

Question 3: It's important for you to be clear about the value you will receive if you implement this type of solution. Do you have a good understanding of the value of this type of solution? How would you define the value?

Question 4: Other organizations that I've worked with have measured the value of <u><describe solution></u> in four main categories <u><list the categories></u>. Do those sound like good categories to classify the value you would expect to receive by taking on this project? If so, what value do you think your organization should/would expect to receive in each area?

> <u>Example</u>: Other organizations that I've worked with have measured the value of implementing a sales force automation solution in the following categories: 1) increased revenue per rep 2) increased forecast accuracy 3) improved close date 4) shorter sales cycles. Do those sound like good categories to you?

<u>Question 5</u>: I imagine your executives will want to know the ROI on this project. How do you typically calculate and communicate a project's ROI?

○ ○ ○
○ ○ ○
○ ○ ○
● ○ ○

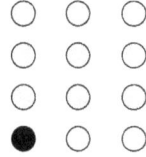

CHAPTER 13:
PAYMENT
QUESTIONS

Definition **Reminder**: The prospect needs to have the underlined budget available to make a purchase. You need to be sure that the money they have to spend is in the ballpark of what is required to purchase your solution so you don't invest a bunch of time chasing the wrong deal. Finally, you need to know the owner of the budget. We will talk about how you influence payment in the Actions section.

Example 1: This is a fairly significant investment. Do you have money set aside to invest in this project?

Example 2: This may not have been on your radar when you were going through the budgeting process at the end of last year. Does someone have money in their budget to cover this? Who?

Example 3: People generally invest somewhere between <u>give a low to hi price range</u> on this type of solution. Are you able to access funds in that range?

Examples 4: Which department pays for our solution varies from company to company. Sometimes the <u>department 1</u> pays for it and sometimes the <u>department 2</u> pays for it. Which department would be responsible for funding this project at your organization?

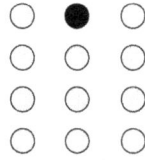

CHAPTER 14:
PROCESS QUESTIONS

Definition **Reminder**: You need to know what <u>steps</u> the buyer will take to make a purchase so you can prepare, adapt and play to your strengths. It is also important to know the expected <u>timeline</u> for completing the steps as well as which <u>people</u> will be participating in each step. We will talk about how you can positively influence their buying process in the Actions section.

<u>Question 1</u>: You've purchased these types of solutions before. What steps does your organization typically go through to evaluate and select vendors for these types of solutions?

Question 2: Who is typically involved in each of the steps you just mentioned?

Question 3: With the companies I've worked with in the past, people in <u>name positions, departments or roles</u> usually get involved in the evaluation process. Is it the same here? Who are those people?

> Example: With companies I've worked with in the past, the CIO, VP of Sales, Sales Managers and a few key salespeople were usually involved in the evaluation process. Is it the same here? Who are those people?

Question 4: There are often several steps that have to be completed after you actually select a vendor...things like committee meetings, legal review, final executive signoff and purchasing approvals. What steps will you have to take after you select the solution you want to purchase?

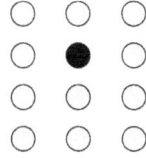

CHAPTER 15:
PREFERENCES
QUESTIONS

efinition Reminder: The buyer needs to be clear about what constitutes an ideal solution, preferably by capturing buying preferences as a list of specific <u>criteria</u>. Criteria are usually more than just features and functions. Other things like vendor reputation, vendor size, other customers, prestige of ownership etc. also come into play. You need to know their buying criteria, as much as possible, before you begin sharing the details about your solution (ie: selling) to make sure you communicate the aspects of your solution that are best aligned with what they need. It is also important to know the <u>weight</u> of importance for each criterion (ie: "must have" vs. "nice to have"). We will talk about how you <u>adjust</u> and <u>align</u> to their preferences in the Actions section.

<u>Question 1</u>: You mentioned that it's important for a solution to have <u><list their buying criteria></u>. Can you give me some additional insight into why those things are important to you?

> <u>Example</u>: You mentioned that it is important for a solution to have automated lead nurturing, mass email blasts and custom reporting. Can you give me some additional insight into why those things are important to you?

<u>Question 2</u>: Many of the companies we work with prefer to have <u><list the buying criteria that are strengths of your solution></u>. How important are those things to you? Are there things that are more important?

> <u>Example</u>: Many of the companies we work with feel that it is important to have automated lead nurturing, mass email blasts and custom reporting. How important are those things to you? Are there things that are more important?

Question 3: Which of the criteria that you mentioned do you feel are most important?

Question 4: Which criteria are so important that you wouldn't buy a solution without it?

Question 5: What other aspects are important for the solution you purchase to include?

○ ○ ○
○ ○ ○
○ ● ○
○ ○ ○

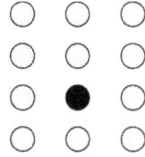

CHAPTER 16:
POSITIONING QUESTIONS

Definition **Reminder**: You need to know how your solution is positioned in relation to your competitor(s) so you can emphasize your <u>strengths</u> and try to minimize your <u>weaknesses</u>. Many prospects are uncomfortable about sharing competitive information so you have to be careful about how you ask positioning questions so they don't shut down on you. People are particularly sensitive to divulging the names of specific competitors. While it's always nice to know who you're up against, you can get what you need without knowing competitor names.

Question 1: You mentioned that <list preferences> are important to you. Based on what you've learned so far, how do you feel that our solution rates in each of those areas?

Get their answer. Then ask:

Question 2: I'm not really concerned about knowing exactly who else you are considering but, I would like to know if any of the other solutions rates higher in any of the areas you just mentioned. If so, which areas? Why?

Question 3: Do you think that our solution is particularly strong on any of your key requirements?

Question 4: I appreciate your honesty and you won't hurt my feelings...is there another solution that you and your team are leaning toward at this time? (If they answer "yes", stay calm and ask the following question.) What do you like about that solution?

Question 5: How did you decide which vendors you would evaluate for this project? Which companies made the list?

○ ○ ○
○ ○ ○
○ ○ ○
○ ● ○

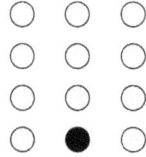

CHAPTER 17:
PROOF
QUESTIONS

efinition Reminder: The buyer needs to have compelling evidence that supports the claims you've made about your solution. It's not enough to simply state that your solution will deliver a particular aspect of value. Instead, you have to provide actual proof of the <u>Payback</u> your solution will provide, how it aligns to their <u>Preferences</u> and how it is <u>Positioned</u> better than your competition. After you provide the proof point, you should validate that the evidence you've provided has instilled confidence in them.

<u>Question 1</u>: One of the things that you mentioned is important to you in your purchase

decision is <u><list a key Preference></u>. As you may recall, I shared that <u><list Proof point about that Preference></u>. Was that useful supporting information?

> Example: One of the things you said is important to you is to work with a company that really takes care of its customers. As you may recall, I shared that 98% of our customers renew their agreements each year. Does that seem like compelling evidence that we take care of our customers? Do you need to know anything else to be comfortable/confident about this?

Question 2: In one of our earlier discussions I mentioned that most of our customers are able to <u><describe results that other customers have achieved></u>. Do you feel confident that we could make that big of an impact on your organization?

> Example: In one of our earlier discussions I shared that most of our customers are able to increase revenue per rep by 10% after implementing our solution. I also provided a case study about XYZ Company that detailed how they actually experienced better results. Do

you feel confident that we could make that big of an impact on your organization?

Question 3: I don't want to assume that you are completely convinced that our solution is the best thing since sliced bread. Is there anything else you need to know to feel comfortable going with our solution?

Question 4: I've shared several quotes from our customers as well as a reference letter that one of customer wrote to me. Based on that information, and the conversations we've had over the past few meetings, do you believe that our solution will meet your requirements?

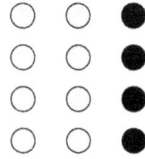

CHAPTER 18:
PEOPLE QUESTIONS

Definition Reminder: Your ultimate job is to convince the most influential people in the account that your solution is best suited to address their needs. As we discussed, the three main roles of the people you need to convince are Recommender, Approver and Influencer. You need to spend <u>time</u> with them, adapt to their <u>personality</u>, uncover their <u>top criteria</u>, know the <u>personal impact</u> the decision will have on them and address any of their <u>concerns</u>. All too often, salespeople don't know whether the key people are for them or against them during a sales cycle. A big reason salespeople don't know is that they don't ask. They don't ask because they are afraid of the answer or they are simply uncomfortable with asking direct questions. You want to know the answer so you can do something about it if it's not good news. Hopefully, these questions will help you see that it is possible to find out this information without feeling awkward or uncomfortable.

Question 1: You guys have been evaluating solutions for quite a while. If you had to decide which solution to go with today, which one would you pick? (Let them answer, then ask this follow-up question.) What are the main reasons why you would go with that solution?

Question 2: I just want to do a quick status check to see where you are with regard to choosing a solution. What is your gut feel about which solution would best fit your needs?

Question 3: It's not always easy to see the differences in these types of solutions. At this point, do you feel that one solution seems better suited to your needs? (Let them answer, then ask this follow-up question.) What has made you feel this way?

Question 4: I'm curious…what's your overall perception of the various solutions you've evaluated so far?

QUESTIONS SUMMARY

Knowing where you stand on a sales opportunity is half the battle. The Opportunity
Dashboard illuminates the key areas to consider
on each sales opportunity. The questions in
chapters 10-18 arm you with everything you need
to capture the most important information on
each dashboard indicator. You can begin using
these questions today to get better insight on
your sales opportunities. Review the Questions
chapters frequently to remind yourself of ways
to frame questions to capture better information. Take time to study the examples that are
provided for each indicator. Then write out your
own questions for each indicator to mold them to
your own speaking style and the solution you are
selling. Commit to studying your own questions

for 30 days so they become easy to recall and use in selling situations. Great questions will provide the information you need to which positions you to take the right actions to improve your probability of winning sales opportunities.

SECTION 3:
ACTIONS

In the previous section, we talked about how to ask questions to get the answers you need for each of the Dashboard indicators. The last and most important thing we need to cover is what you should do if the information you receive on any Dashboard indicator is negative or incomplete. When using Dashboard Selling, your primary job is to influence each of the indicators in your favor. There are many factors that affect the psychology behind influencing people, because we humans are pretty complex little creatures. For the sake of keeping this book clear and concise, I won't inundate you with the complexities of human psychology. Instead, we'll just focus on defining key Actions that have been proven to influence buyers and accomplish your objectives.

● ○ ○
○ ○ ○
○ ○ ○
○ ○ ○

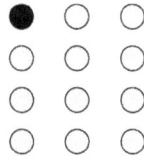

CHAPTER 19:
PAIN ACTIONS

To get the "green light" on the Pain indicator, you need to uncover the issues that the prospect is encountering as well as the impact that those issues are having on the prospect's organization and the people who work there. What should you do if the prospect doesn't have any pain or isn't willing to admit their pain?

First, if they truly don't have any pain, run for the hills. You'll waste a ton of your precious selling time with someone who is just willing to talk. Who knows why? Maybe they're lonely. Maybe they're bored. Maybe they like staying informed. Just move on if they don't have pain.

More often, prospects do have pain but they don't want to admit it to a commissioned salesperson with dollar signs in their eyes. Here's where you can get to work. Your job is to <u>uncover</u> and <u>inflame</u> the pain. With the right actions, you can turn a small spark into a raging forest fire that the prospect will decide must be put out.

ISSUES

<u>Action 1</u>: One great way to inflame pain is to reference one of the prospect's competitors that is more advanced in that area or who has already resolved the issue. No one likes to hear that their competitors are kicking their tail. For example, if you are selling to Company A, you might say "I read an article about Company B growing their business about 10% by using an automated lead nurturing system".

<u>Action 2</u>: Another great way is to share a story about one of your customers who was in a similar situation before they started working with you. Initially they thought their problem wasn't too bad but after further investigation they found that it was actually a very significant issue that they had to resolve.

<u>Action 3</u>: Using reverse psychology can also be effective when handling prospects who won't admit to having any pain. For example, you could make the following statement: "It must be nice to work in a stress-free, problem-free environment. You're the first company I've ever seen that doesn't have at least one or two issues in this area." Prospects will usually react to this type of statement by opening the door to at least a few honest comments about the problems they're encountering. They might say something like "well it's not perfect around here" which opens the door for you to ask what could make it perfect.

<u>Action 4</u>: Most people are terrible at looking into the future, so get the prospect to consider the consequences of not resolving the issue. You can be a tremendous asset to your prospects by helping them visualize the future and what might happen if they don't take action to resolve their problem now. Encourage your prospect to consider both the personal and company-wide impact of acting or not acting.

<u>Action 5</u>: Emphasizing the potential Payback of solving the problem based on your previous experience and or the facts the prospect has

shared with you about their situation can also be effective. Defining Payback within a specific time period (ex: dollars per day, week, month) can help elevate the importance of taking action sooner than later. For example, a sales force automation software sales person might say "our software typically improves revenue by 3-7%. With your monthly revenue of $200k, that would be an additional $6k to $14k per month just from upgrading your solution".

IMPACT

Once you uncover <u>issues</u> it is extremely important to find out how those issues are impacting their organization. A laundry list of issues without their identified impact is like carrying a gun without the bullets. So ask questions about key business drivers such as customers, competitors, employees, goals, financials and risk. Following are several examples:

How is this issue impacting the service you provide to your <u>customers</u>?

Do you feel like your <u>competitors</u> are doing a better job in this area?

How is this impacting your company's (department's) <u>goals</u>?

What is the <u>financial</u> impact of this issue?

This issue must be impacting your <u>employees</u>… what effect do you think it is having on them?

If you uncover pain, inflame pain and clearly identify how the pain is impacting the company's primary concerns (i.e. "business drivers"), you've fulfilled the first indicator in Dashboard Selling.

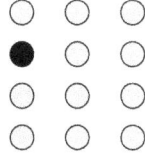

CHAPTER 20:
PRIORITY ACTIONS

Limited time, money and people prevent organizations from solving all of their pains. You know something is a priority when three things happen: 1) a person is taking <u>ownership</u> of the problem 2) an official <u>project</u> has been initiated by someone with the appropriate level of power and 3) the project has a <u>deadline</u>. Here are a few things you can do if you've identified a clear pain but the prospect indicates that it is not a priority.

<u>Action 1</u>: Your first move is to go back to inflaming Pain and illuminating Payback. Pain and Payback are your two best friends in this case. As we said earlier, mentioning your prospect's

competitors is a great way to inflame pain. Bringing the prospect's personal impact into the equation can help too. How could they personally benefit from solving the Pain (ex: promotion). Conversely, how will they be harmed if they don't solve the Pain (ex: continued frustration)?

Action 2: Another way to try to drive your project to the top of the priority list is to attach it to another higher priority project. If the prospect says your project isn't a top priority, your first question should always be "what ARE your top priorities?" Depending on what they tell you, you might be able to connect your project to something else that is on their front burner. Many times, prospects feel like they need to solve one problem before they move on to the next problem. However, there are plenty of scenarios where there are benefits to solving two problems at the same time. You just need to help them see how they can kill two birds with one stone.

Action 3: When a project doesn't have a clear deadline, you can help elevate the need to resolve the pain by quantifying the negative impact of not solving the problem and its cumulative cost on a daily, weekly or monthly basis. The impact could be poor financial results, lost customers, fewer won customers, employee attrition, productivity, etc. Clarifying the quantitative impact can help solidify the need to establish a deadline.

Action 4: Sometimes prospects are concerned that they don't have the time to invest in implementing a new solution. You can help eliminate this mental barrier by minimizing the prospect's perception of the time and effort that will be required to implement your solution. In addition, you can demonstrate how people from your company will absorb most of the time required to implement your solution so the prospect's people can stay focused on other higher priority projects.

.

○ ○ ○
○ ○ ○
● ○ ○
○ ○ ○

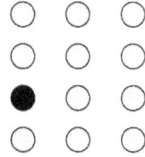

CHAPTER 21:
PAYBACK ACTIONS

As you recall, it's important for a prospect to clearly understand the Payback they will receive by resolving a particular Pain. If they're not clear on the Payback, it is very likely that the project will lose steam before they make a purchase. You'd be surprised at how many times prospects aren't really as savvy as you think and they don't really have a solid grasp of the Payback on a given project. That's why salespeople end up spending their time pounding their heads against the wall when sales cycles end up being way longer than they initially expected. What can you do to be sure your prospects are rock solid on Payback?

Here are a few ideas.

Action 1: Give the prospect case studies and customer testimonials that demonstrate the measurable, tangible Payback you've delivered to other similar organizations. When conveying them, don't just hand them (or email) the document to read. Instead, take the time to walk through the key points with them and bring the case study to life with examples and anecdotes. Make it real. They won't get that three-dimensional understanding if they have to read it on their own.

Action 2: Create a simple but powerful ROI document that captures a reasonable "before & after" snapshot of their situation. It doesn't have to be overly complex or super sophisticated. Something that captures and compares relevant data on things like revenue, expenses, time spent on a function or process, number of employees or man-hours required to accomplish a task, equipment utilization rates, etc. This ROI document should capture "quantitative" payback… dollars and cents…things you can actually hang a number on. You should be able to use relatively conservative percentages to produce a solid ROI. If you can't, I'd suggest that you find something else to sell. When you give your key contact an ROI document, you help them become more effective at selling internally for you. You also build favor with them in the process because you make them look good by arming them with professional tools.

Action 3: Provide an article by an industry expert, analyst or other credible third-party that discusses the value of solutions like yours. It's great if they mention your company by name, but it can still be effective if it doesn't. Sometimes an expert's endorsement of the value of solutions in your space can be just enough to turn your prospect into a buyer.

Action 4: Don't forget to emphasize the "qualitative" Payback of your solution too. Remember, people make buying decisions emotionally and they justify them rationally. You can trigger their emotional buying button with qualitative Payback like reduced frustration, better information, better perception of boss, easier to complete a task, status of using your solution, resume builder, etc.

Action 5: If you've <u>documented</u> and discussed the <u>quantitative</u> and <u>qualitative</u> value of your solution, the last thing you need to do to get the green light on the Proof indicator is to <u>validate</u> that the prospect accepts the data as legitimate. Remember, everything in Dashboard Selling is based on the prospect's feedback.

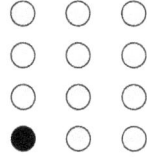

CHAPTER 22:
PAYMENT
ACTIONS

I t's a tough place to be when you have a prospect
that has a problem, sees the value in solving it,
but doesn't have any money. Rather than give up,
take a minute to walk around to the prospect's
side of the desk (metaphorically speaking) and
work to find a solution for their Payment problem. Three things must exist for the Payment
indicator to light up in your favor. The prospect
must have <u>budget</u> to spend that is in the <u>ballpark</u>
of your solution's price and you should know the
budget's <u>owner</u> since he or she wields the biggest influence on your outcome. You can take a
couple of approaches to this challenge.

Action 1: First, help your main contact win the internal support they need to obtain funds for your project. For example, provide a cost justification document that will convince management of the need to invest in solving the problem. Letting your Recommender approach the Approver without a clear message about Payback is a great way to kill a deal. Equipping them to win the internal battles not only improves your chances of making the sale, it'll also strengthen your relationship for follow-on deals.

Action 2: Consider offering an alternate payment plan. Perhaps they could make a partial payment upfront then pay the remaining balance over time.

Action 3: You could "piece-meal" your solution, delivering it in phases so they can pay for and receive part of it now and the remainder later.

Action 4: Explore the possibility of signing the agreement now with an effective date in the future. Moving the cost (and delivery) into a different budgeting period could work better.

<u>Action 5</u>: Depending on the nature of your solution, you could also explore third-party leasing options.

<u>Action 6</u>: Suggest that they look for unused funds in other department's budgets.

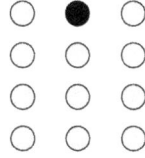

CHAPTER 23:
PROCESS ACTIONS

If the prospect has an unclear or ill-defined buying process, don't head down the road to nowhere with them. If they don't know <u>how</u> the purchase is going to be made, there's a good chance they don't know <u>if</u> the purchase can be made. You'll be doing yourself (and the prospect) a favor by helping them nail down their buying process beforehand. Remember, to turn the Process indicator into a "green light" you need to know:

a) The <u>steps</u> in their buying process.
b) The <u>people</u> who will be involved in each step.
c) The <u>timeline</u> associated with each step.

Here are a few ideas of how you can impact the Process indicator.

Action 1: Tell the prospect that you would hate to see them waste their time evaluating solutions if it's not going to work-out for them. Suggest that they ask their boss (or their boss' boss) what would need to happen for them to purchase a solution to solve their problem. It's better to find out now before you've invested a ton of time on the account.

Action 2: Suggest the typical steps that other prospects have taken and get them to affirm or deny that those steps would work for their organization.

Action 3: Tell the prospect the roles of the people who are usually involved in each of the common steps and ask if they agree that those people should be involved at their organization. If they agree, ask for the names of the people in each position.

Action 4: It can be very helpful to document their buying process and share it with the prospect. This gives you something to use to hold them accountable to the steps and timeline they outlined. You can refer back to it as the sales cycle progresses to make sure things are still on track with the original plan. If things change with the original plan, this might alert you to a problem you need to address. Without knowing the steps they plan to take, you may not even realize you are losing the deal. If you get frustrated by handholding clients, get over it, or you may miss out on sales that just needed you to put on your coaches hat for a while.

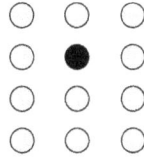

CHAPTER 24:
PREFERENCES
ACTIONS

To make a strategic purchase, a buyer must have clearly defined their Preferences which often take the form of buying criteria or requirements. Buying decisions are usually delayed until there is agreement on Preferences. You can help expedite the process by helping the buyer define their Preferences. Following are the things you must do to satisfy the Preferences indicator:

1. Identify their buying <u>criteria.</u>
2. Determine the <u>weight</u> of each criterion.
3. Try to <u>adjust</u> their criteria in your favor.
4. <u>Align</u> your solution to their preferences.

Here are several actions you can take to Adjust and Align criteria once you've uncovered them using the Questions provided in Chapter 15 (Preferences Questions).

ADJUST

Try one or more of these approaches to adjust their buying criteria:

<u>Action 1</u>: Suggest they consider whether other criteria (that happen to be your strengths) are more important than some they have listed.

<u>Action 2</u>: Reference the criteria most frequently used by other customers who chose your solution.

<u>Action 3</u>: Reference an industry article, analyst or other credible third party who states what buyers should consider when purchasing your type of solution.

ALIGN

Some salespeople are pretty good at being "consultative" and uncovering buyer preferences, but fail to connect the dots between the prospect's

preferences and the solution's matching features. Burying a prospect in a boilerplate litany
of irrelevant features will only confuse and annoy
them. Great sellers tailor their message for each
prospect based on their buying criteria. Try one
of the following approaches to adjusting the
criteria in your favor:

<u>Action 1</u>: Walk through their criteria one-by-one
and communicate how your solution aligns to each
of their criteria. Don't give them a "canned pitch".
You wouldn't tell a man dying of thirst about how
great water is for washing cars or making rainbows,
so stick to what's relevant to your prospect and
their Preferences. Raving about the other features
makes for fine post-sale conversation.

<u>Action 2</u>: After you finish explaining how your
solution addresses each of their Preferences,
ask them how they feel your solution rates on
each Preference (ex: strong, average, weak).
Encourage them to be honest with their rating
because you want to make sure you address anything that they feel is weak.

<u>Action 3</u>: After you've asked for their perception
of how your solution rates on each Preference,

reinforce the areas where you're strong and re-explain your solution's merits in areas the prospect perceives as a weakness.

Action 4: As you walk through each of their criteria, give them examples of other customers who have benefited from that particular aspect of your solution.

Action 5: After you explain a particular aspect of your solution, ask them if they see how that addresses one of their specific buying criteria. Pay careful attention as they listen and respond because their mood and body language usually indicates areas of discomfort that you need to address.

To turn the Preferences indicator green, the buyer must acknowledge that your solution meets their top criteria. If you still have weaknesses after addressing each criteria, the Preferences dial would be yellow. If you have lots of problems, the dial should be red which means you might need to invest your selling time on another opportunity.

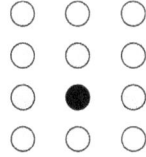

CHAPTER 25:
POSITIONING
ACTIONS

Positioning is all about how your solution compares to the competition because buyer perceptions (not reality) are the only thing that matter. Don't worry if your prospect is reluctant to identify your competition. Just stay focused on addressing any aspects of your solution that are apparently underwhelming in comparison to other solutions they're considering. Don't give up on emphasizing your areas of strength and minimizing the real impact of what your prospect considers a shortcoming. Try a few of these approaches to address any weaknesses you uncover.

<u>Action 1</u>: First, don't get defensive. I could wall-paper my house with greenbacks if I had a dollar for every time I heard a salesperson blast back at a prospect with a litany of whiny "but we're really good at blah, blah, blah too". Getting worked up does more harm than good. Trust me. Just stay calm and objective.

<u>Action 2</u>: Next, simply ask "what is it that has given you the impression that our solution is weak in that area?" You may realize they misunderstood something you said and you can simply clarify. Or you may discover that your competitor has been spreading some FUD ("fear, uncertainty & doubt") or, it may originate in something they read or heard. In any case, knowing the origin of the misperception is important.

<u>Action 3</u>: Ask if they would be <u>open</u> to having you explain that aspect of your solution again. It is good to use the word "open" when you ask the question because people usually don't want to appear "closed" to new ideas. Once they confirm that they're willing to listen, do your best to reframe that aspect of your solution in a manner that will be most compelling to them based on the things they've shared with you.

Action 4: Reiterate and emphasize your solution's strengths that the prospect has already acknowledged using any of the following approaches:

- Recap the strengths that the buyer has acknowledged in the introduction and closing remarks of your sales presentation.
- Bullet-point the strengths on a slide in your presentation.
- Reference a customer quote that talks about that aspect of your solution.
- Reference an article that identifies that aspect of your solution as a strength.

The Positioning indicator is green when the buyer explicitly communicates that another vendor isn't in a better position to win their business.

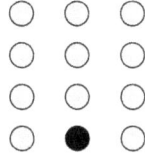

CHAPTER 26:
PROOF ACTIONS

To be effective, you must have credible evidence to back up your claims specifically as they relate to Payback, Preferences and Positioning. Don't make the Proof step a one-time event in the sales cycle where you pound them over the head with an array of "supporting evidence". Remember that people form perceptions over time and you need to offer evidence at each prospect interaction so they end up with a positive perception of you, your company and your solution. If you hang onto your proof until the end, planning to use it like the grand finale at a fireworks show, you may never get to light that fuse, especially if your lack of proof has formed a bias against your solution. Since it's very difficult to change a person's perception once it is solidly formed, consider taking one or more of the following actions to provide proof for buyers.

Action 1: The first rule of providing Proof is to integrate small nuggets of Proof into each of your interactions with the prospect.

Action 2: Quotes from satisfied customers are gold, but they can lose their value if you mistreat them. Instead of just lobbing them around or slapping them on your presentation slides as an afterthought, make them the payoff of a story. Provide some color commentary and details on their industry peer who made the statement and describe the situation their organization was in before they implemented your solution. When you make the quote sound like the big deal it is, it can tilt the balance in your favor.

Action 3: Share your own personal experiences with your customers. When a prospect hears the intimate details of another customer's situation before and after implementing your solution can be far more effective than a glossy case study about some random customer in a far off place the prospect may never visit. Tell them about the people you worked with. Describe the evaluation process they went through and some of the comments they made afterward. Bring the story to life. An additional benefit to this approach is that it not only increases the confidence in your solution but also helps boost your own personal credibility at the same time.

<u>Action 4</u>: Using personal letters of reference has become a lost art. In the old days, before computers, websites, email marketing, blogs and social media, every great salesperson had a binder containing their arsenal of sales tools. The single best sales tool a salesperson had was a letter written by one of their customers making comments about their experience working with the salesperson and their company and their satisfaction with the solution. Few salespeople get these personal letters from their customers today. If you get them and use them, you will stand head and shoulders above the next guy and provide the Proof your buyers need to say "yes" to your solution.

<u>Action 5</u>: If your company has a marketing department, you can always use the tools they provide such as case studies, white papers, analyst quotes, industry articles, video testimonials,

product demonstrations, etc. When possible, try to elevate the buyer's perception of the importance of the information contained in the tool by delivering and discussing it in person. Highlight key sentences or phrases that are particularly relevant to the prospect.

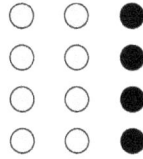

CHAPTER 27:
PEOPLE ACTIONS

The last, and most important, thing you have to do in each sales opportunity is to gain the support of the key people within the account. All the stars may be aligned on the rest of the Dashboard but you can still lose the deal if you don't win over the people with the greatest influence on the decision. While there are a million-and-one things you can do to gain the favor of the people you're selling to, we've boiled them down into five key actions you should focus on.

Before we jump into the five key actions, we need to mention one obvious, but not always followed, rule. It should go without saying, but not saying anything about it would be a disservice to you, the reader. This obvious, base-level rule is this:

<u>buyers have to like you</u>. I know, I know...it seems pretty simple, but it makes a huge difference in the process.

I could list a bunch of things you can do to get people to like you. For example, you should:

Smile

Follow-up promptly

Be courteous

Be professional

Etc., etc.

To paint the lines on your road more clearly, though, it's likely more useful to list the things NOT to do. This list would zero in on the things that have the greatest impact on your "likability". We should be able to say "treat others as you would like to be treated" and that should provide a clear enough guideline, but a lot of salespeople have been treated in odd, harsh and irregular ways for so long in this tough business that one can lose touch with what is "normal" treatment.

Maybe a better statement would be "treat buyers the way they want to be treated" but some salespeople might struggle with that one too.

To make it a little clearer, here is a short list of "don't dos" to help guide your interactions with prospects and buyers:

Don't hound them to the point of obsession.

Don't lie to them. They'll usually figure out the truth at some point.

Don't try to FORCE them to do something they don't want to do. Instead, you should try to persuade them to WANT to do it. It takes a little more thought and creativity on your part but that's what you're getting paid for.

Don't make a promise you can't/don't keep.

Don't blatantly bash your competition. Instead, talk about the positive aspects of your solution. Tell them what makes your company stand out in a crowd.

I think you get the idea...

Okay…now that the ground rules are out of the way let's dig into the five key actions you can take to gain the support of people in an account. Remember, your job is to influence each person in your direction. These are proven ways to influence people.

Time

First, you have to spend time with them. When you look at your Dashboard, the first question you should ask is "how much time have I spent with that person"? If it is "none" or "little" then you should come up with a plan to spend time with them. It's very hard to influence someone who you don't interact with.

Top Preferences

Identify and discuss each person's top preferences. As we said, each person has a different opinion about which Preferences are most important. Person 1 may care most about Preferences A, B & C while Person 2 may care most about Preferences D & E. Once you know each person's Top Preferences, you should focus the majority of your discussion with that person on those Preferences. You can mention the other Preferences that are important to the rest of the organization, but gear about 80% of your conversation toward those Preferences at the top of that person's list. Your choice of topics will have a big impact on your influence.

Concerns

We've all been guilty of ignoring or avoiding concerns that a buyer may have about purchasing our solution. Sometimes we mentally sweep their concerns under the rug hoping that they'll just go away or that we'll somehow win the deal in spite of the buyer's concerns. Take a good look in the mirror and ask yourself how many times you were able to win a deal when buyers had major concerns about your solution. It just doesn't happen. When buyers are concerned, they either postpone the decision until they can resolve their concerns or they buy from your competitor. The best way to eliminate the issues, after you've asked the buyer what concerns they have, is to hit them straight on by taking the following steps:

<u>Step 1</u>: First...do not get defensive. Simply, calmly ask them what has caused their concern.

Step 2: Explain that aspect of your solution again in the event they'd misinterpreted something you said and a clarification will resolve the issue.

Step 3: Share stories of other customers who had the same or similar concerns and how you were able to overcome them. If necessary, give them a reference to speak to about it.

Step 4: If possible, demonstrate that aspect of your solution to show them there's no reason for concern.

Step 5: If you go through the first four steps and they are still concerned, invite them to speak with one of your existing customers.

Sometimes people's concerns are warranted. It's entirely possible that your solution is actually weak in a particular area, so be honest and ac-knowledge the weakness. Acting like it doesn't exist makes you seem either stupid or dishonest and nobody wants to do business with anyone fitting that description. Try to minimize the sig-nificance of their area of concern and balance out the negative by emphasizing key strengths of your solution.

Personal Impact

Given the pressures of selling, one can get so focused on business that the human element is forgotten. Every prospect has personal goals and motivations that affect their decisions at work. Whether they want to hold onto their job, impress their boss, get that promotion and raise or position themselves for another job, people are pursuing something. The sooner you figure out what's driving your prospects, the greater your influence will be. When they answer your question, "how will this project personally affect you," you can connect their responses to those motivations and show that your solution will help them.

Personality

One of the single best ways to gain the favor of another person is to "talk their language". Some people are naturally intuitive, able to pick up on each buyer's nuances and adapt without thinking, while others, maybe you, have to really work at it. In that case, a repeatable system can help you identify buyer personalities and adapt to them. Improving your effectiveness in this area is not as hard as it seems.

If you have time to read all the studies and books written about personality profiling, go for it. However, if you're time-limited and want results sooner, try a simple, sales-friendly method we developed to help you read people and adjust their personality. Called the READ method, it is a simple way to categorize people into one of four major personality types. Each can help you tailor your communication style to suit the situation and the person making the buying decision.

Results
Expressive
Assurance
Details

Results-oriented people don't care about anything but getting things done and will happily mow down anyone or anything standing in their way. Also known as "type A" or "in your face" they will try to make you retreat and cower. The only response they respect is boldness, so be direct with them while focusing on the Dashboard's Payback indicator. They don't care how stuff works, they just want to know what it will do for them. Before you meet with them, know their

Payback then get to the point. Be direct and focus on Payback.

Expressive-oriented people like to work with others to get things done. Great team leaders and positive motivators, they're usually very friendly, willing to share information with you including the details of their personal life. Relationship-driven, Expressive people will be impressed by the names of your marquee customers and will be inspired to choose solutions that other influential companies or people are using. You'll make great headway with them if they understand the prestige or status associated with your solution.

Assurance-oriented people are cautious, risk-averse people who don't like change. Their quiet demeanor will likely require you to fish information out of them. They respond best to opportunities that they perceive to have minimal risk. They are motivated by the desire to minimize change in their daily routine, so be sure they know that your solution will be a seamless addition to their life, guaranteed to deliver as promised.

Detail-oriented people are also easy to spot because they're the ones asking for tons of detailed information. Since the typical sales-person doesn't usually like details, we tend to avoid these types, but we can build a strong relationship by providing all the documentation they're requesting. Otherwise, they'll rapidly develop mistrust. If you can't deliver the details they need, connect them with someone else in your organization (i.e. product specialist, subject matter expert) who can provide the details, speak their language and instill the confidence they need to say yes to your solution.

If you do these five simple things, you will be significantly more effective at gaining the support of the key people within each of your opportunities. You can also feel confident that you are probably making a better impression than your competitors' salespeople.

ACTIONS
SUMMARY

Having several predefined actions you can take to improve the status of each Dashboard indicator will help you react faster, with better results. As you put the recommended actions into practice, you will no doubt find ways to adapt them to suit your needs. You probably have some of your own actions that you already use today. I encourage you to write down additional associated actions that you come up with so you don't forget them. Otherwise, atrophy can set in and hinder your skills development. Feel free to write in additional actions you've found to be effective within each of the relevant chapters so you can refer back to them and have everything in one place. Refer back to the Action chapters in this book regularly to remind yourself how to respond and act to have a greater impact on each Dashboard indicator.

.

SUMMARY

Ok...that's it. The fastest, easiest way to systematically improve your sales results.

But it's all worthless if you don't do one thing.

Use it!

You can't just KNOW about these concepts.

You have to actually USE them.

Learn the DEFINITIONS.

Ask the QUESTIONS

And take the ACTIONS for each Dashboard indicator and you will enjoy greater sales success.

Quick Opportunity Assessment

The diagram below provides one simple question you can ask yourself to determine where you stand on each indicator.

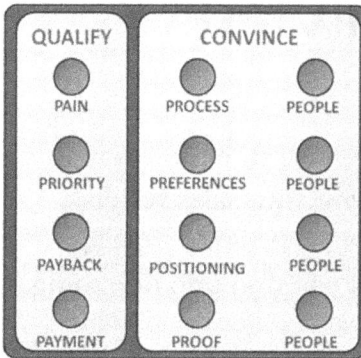

PAIN: Does the prospect have a significant pain that you can eliminate?

PRIORITY: Has the prospect said they are going to solve the problem now?

PAYBACK: Does the prospect know the value of solving the problem?

PAYMENT: Does the prospect have the money necessary to purchase the solution?

PROCESS: Has the prospect told you exactly what they must do to purchase a solution?

PREFERENCES: Is your solution aligned well to the prospect's requirements for a solution?

POSITIONING: Is there another solution provider who is in a better position to win?

PROOF: Have you given the prospect ample evidence of the Payback your solution will provide and the alignment of your solution to their Preferences?

PEOPLE: Has each person indicated that they want your solution?

Detailed Opportunity Assessment

Below is a more detailed list of questions that will help you drill down to the next level on each Dashboard indicator. These questions clarify the nuances of each indicator with more specificity. Asking yourself these questions on each of your deals will give you total clarity about which indicators you need to address. Then use the Questions and Actions described in the previous chapters to address each element.

QUALIFY

Pain
- Has the prospect acknowledged that there are <u>issues</u> that are causing them significant pain?
- Do you know the <u>cause</u> of each issue?

- Do you know how the pain is <u>impacting</u> their key business drivers (customers, competitors, employees, partners, goals, financials, risk, etc.)?

Priority
- Has a person within the organization taken <u>owner</u>ship of solving the pain?
- Has someone with the appropriate power initiated an official <u>project</u> to solve the problem?
- Does the project have a <u>deadline</u> for completion?

Payback
- Have you identified the <u>quantitative</u> and <u>qualitative</u> value your solution would provide to the prospect?
- Have you given the prospect a <u>document</u> that summarizes the value they can expect to receive by solving the problem?
- Has the prospect <u>validated</u> that they believe they will actually receive the Payback that is outlined in the summary document?

Payment
- Has the prospect indicated that they have <u>budget</u> available for the project?

- Is their budget in the <u>ballpark</u> of the amount required for your solution?
- Do you know the <u>owner</u> of the budget?

If these four things exist, you have a qualified opportunity. If not, you need to make sure you continue to try to fill in the "holes" on these indicators. You probably won't slam on the brakes and eject from the opportunity but you should work hard to turn the red lights to green lights. If you don't, they will most likely come back to bite you. You may spend weeks, months or even years working with a prospect only to find that they never purchase a solution.

CONVINCE

Process
- Has the buyer shared all of the <u>steps</u> that they will take to evaluate and select a vendor?
- Has the buyer told you which <u>people</u> will be involved in each step?
- Has the buyer told you the <u>timeline</u> associated with each step and the final purchase?

Preferences
- Has the buyer shared the buying <u>criteria</u> they will use to evaluate solutions?
- Do you know the <u>weight</u> of each criterion ("must have" vs. "nice to have")?
- Have you tried to <u>adjust</u> the criteria in your favor?
- Have you communicated/demonstrated how your solution <u>aligns</u> to their criteria?
- Has the buyer <u>validated</u> that they believe your solution aligns to each of their criteria?

Positioning
- Do you know the buyer's perception of the <u>strengths</u> and <u>weaknesses</u> of your solution and your competitors' solutions?
- Have you <u>emphasized</u> your strengths and <u>minimized</u> your weaknesses?
- Has the buyer indicated that a competitor is in a better Position to win?

Proof
- Have you given evidence that your solution will actually deliver the <u>Payback</u> you communicated?
- Have you demonstrated how your solution aligns to their most important <u>Preferences?</u>

- Have you substantiated any claims you've made regarding your <u>Positioning</u> versus your competitors?
- Have you <u>Validated</u> that the prospect accepts the Proof sources you've provided?

People
- Have you <u>identified</u> the four most important people in the account (Approver, Recommender and the 2 biggest Influencers)?
- Have you spent significant <u>time</u> with each of the top four people?
- Have you determined the <u>personality</u> type of each person and adapted your communication style to them?
- Do you know the <u>top buying criteria</u> (Preference) of each person and are you focusing most of your communication on those areas?
- Have you proactively solicited their <u>concerns</u> about choosing your solution and attempted to resolve those concerns?
- Do you know the <u>personal impact</u> of this decision and are you trying to align your solution in light of that knowledge?
- Has the person indicated that they <u>endorse</u> the decision to purchase your solution?

- Do you have a <u>champion</u> that is actively promoting your solution?

These questions should help you remember the definition of each indicator and keep you focused on the important aspects of each indicator.

If you have the discipline to use Dashboard Selling, you will see your results improve. It's that simple. After just a few weeks of using the dashboard, you will have each of the indicators burned into your brain. You'll see the Opportunity Dashboard in your mind and automatically recall each indicator as you are tackling your daily sales tasks. Before you know it, you will be instinctively asking the questions to capture the information for each of the elements in the dashboard. When you uncover elements that are still "red", you will automatically respond in the appropriate manner to improve your situation. There's no better way to become more effective at selling than viewing each sales opportunity through the same lens and evaluating each opportunity with the same measuring stick. Viewing every important variable related to each of your sales opportunities on a single page and having predefined Questions and Actions for each indicator will catapult you to greater levels of success.

GETTING STARTED

The last thing to do is determine how you will actually implement Dashboard Selling into your daily selling activities. If you don't use it all day, every day, on every sales opportunity, it won't provide the maximum impact. It's kind of like having a gas gauge in your car that you never look at. Having the concepts in your head is one thing. Plotting your opportunities on an actual Dashboard is quite another. It forces you to be honest with yourself about the state of your deals.

There are two main tools you need to get started: the Opportunity Dashboard™ and the Situation Summary™ document. Following is a description and sample of each.

Opportunity Dashboard

The Opportunity Dashboard provides a quick and convenient place for you to capture and assess information about a specific sales opportunity. It also helps you remember what to ask when you are in the heat of battle (ie: talking to a hot prospect). The Opportunity Dashboard works as a reference document making it easier to share the most relevant information with your manager and other team members who may assist you on your sales opportunities. The Dashboard makes it is easy to see where you stand on the opportunity and what you need to do to win it.

As you can see below, there are two main sections of the Dashboard. First is a rating for each Dashboard indicator. You can fill in the rating as you make progress on each element (Blank if it's negative, "P" if it's partially completed and "Y" if it's positive). Second is a detail area where you make notes of the information the prospect shares that is relevant to that indicator. This allows you to quickly retrieve relevant information in the future and accurately assess your opportunities. You should fill your notebook, briefcase and/or desk drawer with plenty of these to pull out anytime you start talking with a new prospect. In addition, you may want to use an electronic version to fill in on a laptop or tablet. The electronic version can be created easily in a spreadsheet, built into your CRM system or downloaded at www.dashboardselling.com.

Area	Description	Rating	Details
Pain	Issues, Causes, Impact	○○ P Y	
Priority	Owner, Project, Deadline	○○ P Y	
Payback	Quantitative, Qualitative, Documented, Validated	○○ P Y	
Payment	Budget, Ballpark, Owner	○○ P Y	
Process	Steps, People, Timeline	○○ P Y	
Preferences	Criteria, Weight, Adjustments, Alignment	○○ P Y	
Positioning	Strengths, Weaknesses, Validated	○○ P Y	
Proof	Payback, Preferences, Positioning, Validated	○○ P Y	
People (A)	Time, Personality, Top Preferences, Concerns, Personal Impact, Status	○○ P Y	
People (R)	Time, Personality, Top Preferences, Concerns, Personal Impact, Status	○○ P Y	
People (I1)	Time, Personality, Top Preferences, Concerns, Personal Impact, Status	○○ P Y	
People (I2)	Time, Personality, Top Preferences, Concerns, Personal Impact, Status	○○ P Y	

P = Partial Y=Yes

Situation Summary™ Document

There are several elements from the Dashboard that, if shared with the prospect, can help you validate that you're on the right track and not making a bunch of inaccurate assumptions. (Imagine that). The tool for doing this is the Situation Summary document. As the following example illustrates, the Situation Summary outlines the following information: Pain ("Issues" & "Impact"), Process (including timeline and People) and Preferences ("Solution"). Different labels are used to be more "prospect friendly". This should be a living, breathing document.

Share the Situation Summary with the information you have after the first call with a new prospect. Then revise and resend as you complete
significant steps in the sales cycle. Review the
document via phone or in person to validate that
you've captured the information they've shared
accurately. You can modify the following tem-
plate to meet your specific needs.

Dashboard Selling Situation Summary™

Date

Dear <Name>,

It was great talking with you today. Thank you
for providing insight into the things <Company
Name> is trying to accomplish in the area of <your
solution type>. Following is a brief summary of
the key information you shared and the process
we agreed to follow to determine whether our
solution is the best for your specific situation.
As we discussed, I will call you on <date/time>
to validate this information and the action plan.
In the meantime, feel free to email me with any

thoughts or changes that you'd like me to make to this document.

Issues (key issues that are impacting your organization)
- abc
- abc
- abc
- abc
- abc

Impact (ways these issues are impacting your organization)
- abc
- abc
- abc
- abc
- abc

Solution (things that you want in a solution)
- abc
- abc
- abc
- abc
- abc

Process (steps you plan to take to evaluate and select a solution)

- <step> <people involved/responsible > (date)
- <step> <people involved/responsible > (date)
- <step> <people involved/responsible > (date)
- <step> <people involved/responsible > (date)
- <step> <people involved/responsible > (date)

Opportunity List

In addition to the Opportunity Dashboard and Situation Summary, it is helpful if you can implement an Opportunity List. The Opportunity List is a single place for you to see a list of all your opportunities and the status of each element. The value of this, beyond the typical information tracked on an opportunity such as close date, amount, probability, and lead source, you have a clear indicator of where the holes are. Seeing it in black and white will make you more conscious of that area so you can improve your Questions and Actions to constantly increase your results. If you use a spreadsheet to track your sales activities, the individual Opportunity Dashboards can feed the Opportunity List so you don't have to reenter the data.   If you use a CRM application, the opportunity list can be created as a report that summarizes the Dashboard Selling fields within your opportunities module.

Dashboard Selling™
Opportunity List

Opportunity Name	Stage	Close Date	Amount	Pain	Priority	Payback	Payment	Process	Preferences	Positioning	Proof	Approver	Recommender	Influencer	Influencer
ABC Company	Qualified	6/10	$ 450,000	Yes	No	Partial	Yes	No	Yes	No	Partial	Yes	No	Yes	Partial
XYZ Company	Presentation	5/11	$ 375,000	No	Partial	No	No	Yes	No	Partial	Yes	Yes	No	Partial	Partial
PDO Company	Proposal	4/30	$ 475,000	Yes	Yes	No	Partial	Yes	Partial	No	No	Partial	Partial	No	No
JMN Company	Proposal	4/15	$ 250,000	No	Yes	Yes	No	Partial	No	Yes	No	Partial	Yes	No	Yes
HIJ Company	Negotiating	3/11	$ 260,000	Partial	No	No	Yes	No	Yes	Yes	Partial	No	No	Yes	Yes

You can create your own versions, build them into your CRM system or go to www.dashboard-selling.com to get access to various tools we've created.

RESULTS
MULTIPLIER

Some folks might have already closed the book and stacked it up on their nightstand thinking the last few pages are just filled with a bunch of meaningless fodder. If you are a person that sticks it out till the end, hoping and expecting to find some final words of wisdom or special nuggets, congratulations. Here's just what you were looking for.

There's no question that using Dashboard Selling will multiply your sales results because it contains the keys to producing better sales results:

a) Knowing how to systematically <u>Assess</u> your sales opportunities.

b) Knowing the <u>Questions</u> that will uncover those things that will influence the buyer.

c) Knowing what <u>Actions</u> you need to take based on the information you uncover.

These are absolutely essential to your success. If you just do them day-in and day-out, you'll be at the front of the pack.

However, there is one other thing you can do to multiply your sales results and it concerns the organ located between your ears. That's right… your brain.

What do you think separates winners and losers? Or even <u>good</u> salespeople from <u>off-the-charts</u> sales people?

Their overall strategy for managing sales opportunities is certainly one thing. That's what Dashboard Selling is designed to address. The other thing is their thoughts. What you think about yourself, your company and your solution makes a huge impact on your sales results. Even more, what you expect and anticipate is usually what you get. If you think you're going to lose the deal, you usually do. It's a weird thing but somehow what we allow our minds to dwell on often ends up happening. If you think everyone is going to reject you, they will. Henry Ford had a great saying "whether you think you can or you think you can't, you are right". There's great wisdom in those words. Given the obstacles he had to overcome in creating a whole new industry, I consider him a trustworthy source.

So, if you want to multiply your results, the last thing you need to do is get your mind right. You have to believe that you are a great salesperson. You have to believe in the value your company provides to its customers. You have to believe that prospects will buy from you. You have to get up each morning and tell yourself it's going to be a great day. Be a "glass half full" person. Speak with enthusiasm. Greet each day with optimism and it usually won't let you down.

To maintain this mindset, you have to stay away from other salespeople who don't share this philosophy. Nine times out of ten, they'll bring you down before you bring them up. Run for the hills when you see them coming. Don't sit in your office or spend long lunches wringing your hands with naysayers.

Get up.

Get out there.

Talk to some customers.

Visualize success (however you define it) and you'll soon taste it.

MAKING A
DIFFERENCE

As you begin to enjoy greater sales success, I hope you'll start thinking about how you can make the world a better place. When you check out of this life, you don't want the only remnant of your existence to be a bunch of old paystubs from your commission checks.

If you're reading this book, you are probably in the top 5% of all income earners in the world, and that accounts for a lot of capital (both financial and personal). Imagine for a moment what could happen if every salesperson used a portion of their time, money and talents to make the world a better place. I believe we could have a tremendous impact on the world, including reducing some of the suffering that is all too common in all too many places. I can't think of any person better equipped to change the world than a salesperson.

If you don't know where to help out, go to www.dashboardselling.com to find ideas.

Just find something to make a dent in and do it…alright?!

ABOUT THE AUTHOR

Robert Beasley is a 20+ year veteran of the sales profession. He is the Founder and CEO of ThisQuarter, a strategy consulting firm based in Austin Texas. ThisQuarter works with CEOs to strengthen their corporate strategies, develop their sales teams and improve their sales processes. Robert has worked with companies in the US, Asia and Europe and has developed methodologies for strategic selling, presenting, negotiating and corporate strategy development. He has a wife, Leslie and four kids, Conner, Kyle, Luke and Lily.